TABLE OF CONTENT

Chapter 1: Introduction..........................
- 1.1 Why Solo Female Travel is Emp...
- 1.2 How to Use This Guidebook... 6
- 1.3 Overcoming Fear: Embracing Solo Travel....................... 8

Chapter 2: Safety First: Tips for Navigating Solo Adventures................11
- 2.1 Pre-Trip Preparations: Planning for a Safe Journey 11
- 2.2 On the Road: Staying Secure in Unfamiliar Environments 13
- 2.3 Personal Safety: Strategies and Techniques for Solo Female Travelers 15

Chapter 3: Inspiring Tales: Stories of Courage and Empowerment 18
- 3.1 The Unstoppable Explorers: Bold Women Who Paved the Way 18
- 3.2 Tales from the Road: Extraordinary Journeys of Solo Female Travelers 19
- 3.3 Breaking Barriers: How Solo Travel Transforms Lives..21

Chapter 4: Connecting with Others: Building Relationships on the Road 24
- 4.1 Making Friends: Overcoming Loneliness and Meeting Like-Minded Travelers 24
- 4.2 Cultural Immersion: Engaging with Local Communities and Building Bridges 26
- 4.3 Solo, Not Solitary: Finding Companionship in Solo Travel 20

Chapter 5: Mind, Body, and Soul: Nurturing Yourself During Solo Journeys 30
- 5.1 Self-Care on the Road: Prioritizing Your Physical and Mental Well-being 30
- 5.2 Inner Reflection: Finding Peace and Balance in Solitude 32

5.3 Mindful Travel: Connecting with Nature and Cultivating Mindfulness 34

Chapter 6: Cultural Sensitivity: Embracing Diversity and Respectful Travel
.... 37

6.1 Cultural Etiquette: Navigating Different Social Norms with Grace 37

6.2 Challenging Stereotypes: Breaking Down Prejudices through Travel 39

6.3 Responsible Tourism: Supporting Local Communities and Preserving Culture 41

Chapter 7: Traveling on a Budget: Making Solo Adventures Affordable 44

7.1 Money-Saving Tips and Tricks: Budgeting and Cutting Costs 44

7.2 Accommodation Hacks: Finding Affordable and Safe Places to Stay 46

7.3 Cheap Eats: Exploring Local Cuisine without Breaking the Bank 48

Chapter 8: Navigating Challenges: Overcoming Obstacles on Solo Journeys 51

8.1 Dealing with Language Barriers: Strategies for Effective Communication 51

8.2 Transportation Dilemmas: Mastering Public Transportation and Getting Around 53

8.3 Solo Female Travel and Its Impact: Facing Societal Pressures and Stereotypes 55

Chapter 9: Embracing the Unknown: Embracing Solo Travel with Confidence 58

9.1 Stepping Outside Your Comfort Zone: Embracing Growth and Adventure 58

9.2 Embracing the Solo Journey: Lessons Learned and Self-Discovery 60

9.3 Empowering Yourself: Embracing the World on Your Own Terms 62

Chapter 1: Introduction

1.1 Why Solo Female Travel is Empowering

Solo Female Travel: Empowering Adventures for Women.

As the modern world becomes more interconnected and globalized, the opportunities for travel have expanded, creating an exciting avenue for personal exploration and growth. In recent years, there has been a significant rise in female travelers who are venturing out on their own, embracing the empowering experience of solo travel. This book delves into the multifaceted reasons behind the empowerment found in solo female travel, providing both inspiration and practical advice for women seeking to embark on their own adventures.

Embarking on solo travel as a woman may seem daunting at first, but the benefits far outweigh any apprehensions. The very act of choosing to explore the world alone is itself a declaration of independence and self-reliance. Traveling solo enables women to escape the constraints and expectations of their societal roles, and immerse themselves in exhilarating experiences that challenge and empower them in unique ways.

One of the most profound reasons why solo female travel is empowering is the liberation it offers from the shackles of fear and insecurity. Society often imposes irrational fears on women when it comes to venturing into unfamiliar territories alone. However, the reality is that the world is not inherently more dangerous for women compared to men. By conquering these fears and embracing solo travel, women are able to refute the notion of vulnerability and reclaim their sense of agency. The confidence gained from navigating unfamiliar places and cultures on their own terms instills a sense of empowerment that transcends the boundaries of their ordinary lives.

Moreover, solo female travel goes beyond personal empowerment; it fosters a sense of communal empowerment among women around the world. By embarking on solo adventures and sharing their stories, female travelers inspire others to break free from societal norms that may restrict their own desires for exploration. Time and again, stories of women conquering their fears, chasing their dreams and learning about the world through solo travel have inspired countless others to follow in their footsteps. The ripple effect of these journeys has created a global community of empowered women who encourage and uplift one another, supporting the notion that women can overcome any obstacle and redefine their own narratives.

Another empowering aspect of solo female travel lies in the opportunity to connect with different cultures on a deeper level. When traveling in a group or with a companion, there is often a reliance on others for interpretation and cultural understanding. However, when women travel solo, they have the freedom to engage with locals on a more intimate level. This allows for a greater appreciation and understanding of diversity, breaking down preconceived notions and prejudices. The ability to communicate, learn from, and form connections with people from all walks of life creates a powerful sense of inclusion and personal growth.

By dismissing societal fears, encouraging a global community of aspiring female travelers, and fostering meaningful connections with diverse cultures, women have the ability to transform their own lives and inspire others to do the same. This guide aims to ignite the adventurous spirit within women, providing practical advice and inspirational stories, so that they may embrace the empowering journey of solo female travel and explore the world on their own terms.

1.2 *How to Use This Guidebook*

Dive into "Solo Female Travel: Empowering Adventures for Women," a comprehensive guide that aims to empower and inspire women to embark on solo travel adventures. This guidebook is designed to provide you with practical advice, safety tips, and encouraging stories to help you explore the world on your own terms. In this section, we will delve into the details of how to effectively use this guidebook to make the most out of your solo travel experiences.

As a traveler myself, I understand the importance of having a trustworthy resource to rely on during your journeys. This guidebook aims to be that reliable companion, offering you valuable insights and guidance every step of the way. Whether you are a seasoned solo traveler or are considering embarking on your first adventure, this book has something for everyone.

To fully leverage the benefits of this guidebook, it's essential to approach it with an open mind and a readiness to embrace new ideas and perspectives. The content within these pages has been meticulously crafted to cater specifically to the unique needs and concerns of solo female travelers. By following the advice provided in this guidebook, you will not only enhance your safety and security while traveling alone but also empower yourself to overcome any challenges that may come your way.

Throughout this guidebook, you will find a wide range of topics that cover various aspects of solo female travel. From tips on packing efficiently to recommendations on choosing the best accommodations, this guidebook aims to address all the practical aspects of your journey. Additionally, you will find firsthand accounts of inspiring women who have successfully embarked on solo adventures, offering you motivation and encouragement to fulfill your own travel aspirations.

One of the key features of this guidebook is its emphasis on safety. We understand that safety concerns can often be a deterrent for women contemplating solo travel. Hence, within the following chapters, you will find comprehensive safety tips, ranging from basic precautions to more advanced strategies for navigating unfamiliar environments. By equipping yourself with knowledge and preparedness, you will be better equipped to handle any situation that may arise during your solo travels.

In addition to practical advice, this guidebook also places a strong emphasis on the emotional and psychological aspects of solo female travel. We understand that embarking on solo adventures can be a transformative experience, offering opportunities for personal growth and self-discovery. In recognizing the significance of these journeys, this guidebook offers guidance on embarking on a spiritually enriching travel experience that goes beyond just checking items off your bucket list.

Finally, to ensure that you can easily navigate through the guidebook, each chapter has been organized in a logical and user-friendly manner. From the to journey planning, accommodation recommendations, and cultural insights, you will find a seamless flow of information throughout this guidebook. Additionally, a comprehensive index at the end of the book will allow you to quickly locate specific information when needed.

By utilizing the practical advice and encouragement provided within this guidebook, you will not only enhance your safety and security but also empower yourself to explore the world on your own terms. Remember, the possibilities are endless, and with this guidebook by your side, you have everything you need to embark on an unforgettable solo travel journey. Happy travels!.

1.3 Overcoming Fear: Embracing Solo Travel

Traveling alone can be a scary prospect for anyone, specifically for women. The fear of the unknown, the worry of safety, and the hesitation to step out of our comfort zones can often hold us back from experiencing the world on our own terms. However, this fear shouldn't stop us from embracing solo travel. By overcoming our fears and taking the plunge into solo adventures, we can not only empower ourselves but also unlock a world of amazing opportunities.

Fear is a natural response to unfamiliar situations, and it can be particularly daunting when it comes to traveling alone. When we think about venturing into a foreign land without the comfort of a familiar companion, self-doubt can creep in. Questions like, "What if something bad happens?" or "Will I be able to handle unexpected challenges?" can flood our minds. It's essential to recognize these fears but not let them hinder our desire for adventure.

Embracing solo travel requires overcoming these fears and reaping the benefits that come with it. Firstly, traveling alone allows us to truly discover ourselves and gain a deeper understanding of our strengths and capabilities. When faced with unfamiliar territory and unexpected obstacles, we are forced to rely solely on ourselves, pushing us to grow and develop in ways we never thought possible.

Furthermore, solo travel empowers us with a sense of independence and self-reliance. It teaches us to trust our intuition and make decisions based on our own judgments. As we navigate through different cultures, languages, and customs, we learn to adapt, communicate effectively, and overcome language barriers. These experiences, although initially daunting, shape us into more confident, resilient individuals.

Overcoming the fear of solo travel also opens up a world of enriching interactions with people from diverse backgrounds. Engaging with locals and fellow travelers not only broadens our perspectives but also provides an opportunity to form meaningful connections. Travelling alone enables us to step out of our comfort zones, fostering personal growth and expanding our horizons.

Although safety is a legitimate concern for any traveler, solo female travelers can take measures to mitigate risks. Researching potential destinations, understanding local customs and laws, and staying vigilant are important aspects of ensuring a safe journey. Additionally, connecting with other solo travelers or joining women-only travel groups can provide a sense of communal support and a network of like-minded individuals.

Throughout this book, you will find a wealth of practical advice and inspirational stories from brave women who have taken the leap into solo travel. Their experiences demonstrate the transformative power of embracing fear and embarking on empowering adventures. By learning from their journeys, you will be armed with the tools, knowledge, and encouragement to set off on your own solo escapades.

Remember, fear is merely a hurdle that can be overcome. By embracing solo travel, you take control of your own experiences, discover your strengths, and create memories that will last a lifetime. Solo female travel is not just a means of exploring the world, but also a path to self-discovery and personal growth. So, pack your bags, overcome your fears, and get ready to embark on an empowering adventure like no other!.

Chapter 2: Safety First: Tips for Navigating Solo Adventures

2.1 Pre-Trip Preparations: Planning for a Safe Journey

Traveling solo as a woman can be an incredibly empowering experience. The freedom, independence, and self-discovery that comes with exploring the world on your own terms is truly unmatched. However, it is essential to prioritize safety during your solo adventures, and that starts with thorough pre-trip preparations. In this section, we will discuss the key aspects of planning for a safe journey, ensuring that you can embark on your adventure with confidence.

First and foremost, before setting off on any solo journey, it is crucial to conduct extensive research on your chosen destination. Familiarize yourself with the local customs, culture, and laws to ensure that you respect and adhere to the norms of the country you are visiting. Understanding the social dynamics and potential risks will not only help you blend in with the locals but also enhance your safety by avoiding any unintentional misunderstandings or unsafe situations.

Equally important is researching the safety situation in your destination. Stay updated on travel advisories issued by government authorities or trusted travel resources, such as the

State Department or travel bloggers. These resources provide valuable information regarding the current political climate, potential health risks, or any specific precautions you need to take. By staying informed, you can make well-informed decisions that prioritize your safety.

While planning your itinerary, be sure to consider your personal safety preferences. Opt for accommodations located in safe neighborhoods, preferably with positive reviews from fellow solo female travelers. Utilize online platforms that provide verified reviews and recommendations to ensure the establishment you choose is reliable and secure. Additionally, select accommodations that offer 24/7 security, as this will provide an added layer of reassurance during your stay.

Pack wisely and efficiently. A lightweight, functional, and secure backpack should be your go-to travel companion. Avoid flashy or expensive-looking luggage that might attract unnecessary attention. Ensure that your backpack is equipped with safety features such as lockable zippers or hidden pockets to safeguard your belongings. It is also advisable to carry a money belt or travel pouch that can be discreetly hidden under your clothing, as this will minimize the risk of losing your valuables or becoming a target for pickpockets.

Before embarking on your journey, make sure to share your travel plans with trusted friends or family members. Provide them with your itinerary, contact information, and copies of essential documents such as your passport, visas, and travel insurance. Regularly check in with them throughout your trip to let them know you are safe and sound. This will not only give you peace of mind but also serve as an additional safety measure in case of any unforeseen circumstances.

By immersing yourself in the local culture, staying informed about travel advisories, choosing secure accommodations, packing intelligently, and sharing your travel plans with loved ones, you can embark on your solo adventures with confidence. Empower yourself with the knowledge and tools necessary to prioritize your safety, and embrace this incredible opportunity to explore the world on your own terms. Safe travels!.

2.2 On the Road: Staying Secure in Unfamiliar Environments

One of the fundamental aspects of staying secure in unfamiliar environments is being aware of your surroundings and maintaining a high level of vigilance at all times. In an unfamiliar environment, it is easy for your senses to become overwhelmed by the new sights, sounds, and experiences. However, it is essential to resist the temptation to let your guard down. By continually assessing your surroundings and staying attentive to any potential threats, you can mitigate the risks and ensure your personal safety.

Furthermore, it is crucial to conduct thorough research before embarking on your solo adventure. Familiarize yourself with the local customs, laws, and traditions of your destination. Understanding the cultural nuances and societal expectations will not only help you blend in, but also prevent any inadvertent actions that may be disrespectful or unsafe. Such knowledge will empower you to navigate through unfamiliar environments with greater confidence and avoid potential pitfalls.

In addition to cultural research, it is paramount to gather information on the regional security situation. Stay updated on current events, travel advisories, and any warnings issued for your destination. Several reliable resources, such as government travel advisories and reputable travel forums, provide vital information that can enhance your situational awareness and aid in keeping you safe during your solo travels.

Equipping yourself with the necessary tools and resources is another crucial aspect of staying secure in unfamiliar environments. Ensure that you invest in a sturdy and reliable backpack or travel bag, designed with built-in safety features such as slash-proof material or lockable compartments. Organizing your belongings in secure pockets or hidden compartments will deter potential thieves and provide peace of mind as you navigate through crowded streets or public transportation.

Moreover, I highly recommend carrying a personal safety alarm or whistle, which can serve as a deterrent or call for help during emergencies. These small yet impactful devices are easy to carry and can attract attention, potentially deterring would-be perpetrators in unfamiliar environments. Additionally, always have a copy of your important documents, such as your passport and identification, securely stored in your accommodation or locked travel bag. This precaution ensures that you have a backup in case of theft or loss, and facilitates the process of obtaining replacements if necessary.

Another invaluable tip for staying secure on the road is to prioritize your personal well-being. This includes maintaining good physical health, practicing self-defense techniques, and trusting your instincts. Prior to embarking on your solo adventure, engage in regular exercise, stay hydrated, and eat nutritious meals to ensure that you are physically prepared for the challenges that lie ahead. Additionally, enrolling in self-defense classes can equip you with the skills and confidence to handle unexpected situations that may arise during your travels.

Trusting your instincts is perhaps one of the most underestimated yet powerful tools in staying secure in unfamiliar environments. As a solo female traveller, you possess intuition and instincts that are finely attuned to potential threats or dangerous situations. By heeding that inner voice, even if it may seem irrational at times, you can circumvent potentially risky scenarios and ensure your personal safety.

By staying aware of your surroundings, conducting thorough research, equipping yourself with necessary tools, and prioritizing personal well-being, you empower yourself to confidently navigate through unfamiliar landscapes. Trusting your instincts and being prepared are key elements that empower women to embark on solo adventures, explore the world, and create enriching experiences on their terms. So, embrace the empowering journey of solo female travel, armed with practical advice and encouragement, and unlock a world of endless possibilities.

2.3 Personal Safety: Strategies and Techniques for Solo Female Travelers

As a seasoned traveler with a passion for exploration, I have had my fair share of incredible experiences on the road. From venturing through ancient ruins to immersing myself in vibrant local cultures, every trip has been an empowering adventure that has broadened my horizons. While traveling solo as a woman can pose unique challenges, I firmly believe that with the right strategies and techniques, personal safety can be assured. In this chapter, I will share some valuable insights on how solo female travelers can confidently navigate the world while prioritizing their personal safety.

First and foremost, it is crucial for solo female travelers to conduct thorough research before embarking on their adventures. Familiarizing oneself with the local customs, traditions, and laws of the destination is of utmost importance. Each country has its own unique set of cultural norms and potential risks that should not be overlooked. With this knowledge, travelers can make informed decisions and better gauge their surroundings, ensuring a safer experience overall.

One effective strategy for personal safety is to maintain a low profile. This means blending in with the local population as much as possible. Dressing modestly and appropriately for the culture not only demonstrates respect but also reduces the likelihood of attracting unwanted attention. As a solo female traveler, it is important to remember that discretion can be a powerful tool in safeguarding one's personal security.

Furthermore, it is advisable to be aware of one's surroundings at all times. This can be achieved by maintaining a focused and observant mindset. Pay attention to the behavior of people around you, trust your intuition, and if something feels off, trust your instincts and remove yourself from the situation. Trusting one's gut feeling is often a reliable indicator of potential danger, and staying vigilant can prevent unfortunate incidents from occurring.

When it comes to accommodations, safety should always be a top priority. Opt for reputable accommodations that have positive reviews and robust security measures in place. Researching the neighborhood where the accommodation is situated can provide valuable insight into its safety profile. Additionally, consider investing in portable safety devices such as door alarms or personal whistles, as they can be effective tools in deterring or notifying others in case of emergencies.

Solo female travelers should also be proactive in their communication and keep loved ones informed of their whereabouts. Sharing information such as hotel addresses, transportation itineraries, and emergency contact numbers can be essential in case any untoward incidents were to occur. Consistent communication with a trusted contact back home not only provides peace of mind but also acts as an extra layer of security.

As a solo female traveler, it is important to strike a balance between independence and seeking assistance when needed. Researching reliable transportation options and mapping out one's routes can aid in having a smoother journey. Utilizing reputable transportation services, such as registered taxis or ride-sharing apps, reduces the chances of falling victim to scams or untrustworthy individuals. Asking for recommendations from fellow travelers, hotel staff, or reputable online platforms can help ensure a safer travel experience.

By conducting thorough research, blending in with the local culture, remaining alert, choosing secure accommodations, staying in touch with loved ones, and utilizing reliable transportation services, solo female travelers can minimize risk and maximize the incredible experiences that await them. Remember, with the right strategies and techniques, the world becomes a playground of possibility, empowering women to explore on their own terms.

Chapter 3: Inspiring Tales: Stories of Courage and Empowerment

3.1 The Unstoppable Explorers: Bold Women Who Paved the Way

One of the extraordinary women highlighted in this chapter is Amelia Earhart, a true pioneer in aviation history. Earhart's courageous solo flight across the Atlantic Ocean in 1932 not only shattered gender barriers but inspired countless women to pursue their dreams fearlessly. Her unyielding determination and unwavering spirit embody the essence of a solo female traveler, provoking awe and admiration in those who dare to challenge societal norms.

Another remarkable explorer featured in this chapter is Gertrude Bell, a fearless adventurer who explored the Middle East during the early 20th century. Often referred to as the "female Lawrence of Arabia," Bell's knowledge and deep respect for the region enabled her to establish strong bonds with local communities and gain invaluable insights into their cultures. Her ability to navigate uncharted territories with remarkable ease and develop a profound understanding of the world around her serves as an inspiration for modern-day female adventurers.

Mary Kingsley, an intrepid explorer of the late 19th century, made significant contributions to scientific knowledge and ethnographic research through her solo expeditions to West Africa. Her unyielding determination and unshakeable curiosity took her to unexplored regions, where she fearlessly immersed herself in the cultures and natural environments. Kingsley's relentless pursuit of knowledge and her commitment to documenting her experiences served as a catalyst for empowering countless women to embrace adventure and curiosity.

Annie Londonderry, a bicycle pioneer, embarked on an unprecedented journey around the world in the late 19th century, becoming the first woman to achieve such a feat. Her audacious expedition not only challenged the societal norms of the time but also shattered stereotypes surrounding women's capabilities and endurance. Londonderry's extraordinary determination and her ability to overcome obstacles demonstrate the unwavering spirit of a solo female traveler.

Their experiences, documented in this chapter, inspire and encourage women to embark on their own journeys, equipped with the knowledge that women have broken barriers and paved the way before them. These women exemplify the indomitable spirit of solo female travel and encourage us to grab hold of our limitless potential as we navigate the world on our own terms.

3.2 Tales from the Road: Extraordinary Journeys of Solo Female Travelers

Through this collection of inspiring stories, readers can delve into the experiences of intrepid women who have embarked on adventurous solo journeys around the world. This section serves as a powerful reminder of the transformative potential of travel and the inherent strength that lies within every woman.

Traveling Off the Beaten Path:

One common thread that binds these extraordinary journeys is the willingness of these solo female travelers to explore beyond the typical tourist destinations. These women, driven by a sense of curiosity and adventure, ventured into remote and unconventional corners of the globe. They took it upon themselves to connect with local communities, immersing themselves in diverse cultures and traditions. These stories truly showcase the transformative magic that can occur when one strays from the well-trodden path.

Challenging Stereotypes and Overcoming Prejudice:

Unquestionably, solo female travelers face unique challenges that require immense resilience and determination. This chapter offers valuable insight into the formidable strength exhibited by these women in defying societal norms and gender biases. By sharing their stories, the travelers reveal their unwavering commitment to smashing stereotypes and challenging cultural perceptions of what women can achieve. In the face of adversity, they demonstrated the power of resilience, inspiring countless other women to overcome their own fears and limitations.

Safety and Empowerment:

Personal safety is a significant concern when embarking on solo adventures, particularly for women. This chapter addresses this concern by sharing practical advice and safety tips, ensuring that women feel informed and prepared prior to taking their journeys. By focusing on strategies to mitigate risk, the book empowers women, allowing them to make informed decisions and approach their travels with confidence.

Cultural Exchange and Human Connections:

Beyond personal empowerment, these extraordinary journeys also highlight the importance of cultural exchange and human connections. Each tale invites readers to discover the profound impact that solo female travelers have on the communities they encounter. By engaging in meaningful interactions and embracing diverse cultures, these women underscore the true essence of travel itself – connecting with others on a deep level, bridging cultural differences, and fostering mutual understanding.

These narratives showcase the power of travel to transform, empower, and inspire women to explore the world on their own terms. Through these tales, readers learn that solo female travel is not simply about crossing destinations off a bucket list but about embracing personal growth and discovering one's inner strength. By using this guide as a source of inspiration, women can ignite their wanderlust and seize the opportunity to empower themselves through travel. After all, the world is waiting to be explored, and women have stories to tell that will embolden others for generations to come.

3.3 Breaking Barriers: How Solo Travel Transforms Lives

There is a profound sense of empowerment that comes with embarking on solo travel. It is a journey that not only takes you to new places physically, but also opens doors to self-discovery, courage, and personal growth. In this section, we dive into the inspiring tales of women who have chosen to embark on solo adventures and how it has transformed their lives in countless ways.

Solo travel has the incredible capability to break down barriers that often hold individuals back from pursuing their dreams and exploring the world on their own terms. It allows women to step outside their comfort zones and take charge of their own destinies, showcasing strength, resilience, and an unwavering determination. Each woman's story is unique, yet they all share a common thread of empowerment that shines through in their experiences.

One of the fundamental barriers that solo travel helps women transcend is the fear of the unknown. Stepping into unfamiliar territory can be daunting for anyone, but solo female travelers conquer this fear head-on. Armed with self-reliance and a thirst for adventure, they confront their anxieties and come out on the other side with a renewed sense of confidence and belief in their abilities. Overcoming this barrier not only transforms lives, but it also leads to personal growth and a greater sense of self.

Another significant barrier that solo travel breaks is societal expectations and stereotypes. Society often imposes expectations on women, dictating how they should behave and what roles they should assume. Solo female travelers challenge these limitations by defying societal norms and proving that they are capable of anything they set their minds to. Through their journeys, they redefine what it means to be a woman, breaking free from the constraints placed upon them and embracing their true selves. This transformative process not only empowers individuals but also inspires others to question and challenge societal norms.

Solo travel also helps women break through the barriers of fear and misconceptions about other cultures and countries. Traveling alone allows individuals to truly immerse themselves in the local culture, fostering deeper connections and understanding. By engaging with people from diverse backgrounds, solo female travelers develop a stronger appreciation for cultural differences, challenging preconceived notions and biases. These encounters shape their perspectives, broaden their horizons, and cultivate empathy and compassion.

Moreover, solo travel provides an opportunity for women to cultivate independence and resilience. Navigating unfamiliar territories, dealing with unexpected challenges, and relying solely on oneself fosters a sense of self-reliance and adaptability. These qualities not only serve women well during their travels but also carry over into all aspects of their lives. They become better problem-solvers, decision-makers, and leaders, equipped with the resilience to overcome obstacles that come their way.

By conquering fears, defying societal expectations, fostering cultural understanding, and cultivating independence, solo female travelers embark on an incredible journey of self-discovery and personal growth. Through their inspiring tales of courage and empowerment, they inspire others to embrace the world on their own terms and reshape their own lives. Solo travel is not just about exploring new destinations, but about embarking on a transformative journey of self-empowerment that can last a lifetime.

Chapter 4: Connecting with Others: Building Relationships on the Road

4.1 Making Friends: Overcoming Loneliness and Meeting Like-Minded Travelers

Traveling can be an incredibly fulfilling and empowering experience, especially when you embark on the journey alone as a solo female traveler. However, one of the challenges one may face when traveling solo is the feeling of loneliness. As human beings, we crave connection and companionship, and being away from our familiar surroundings can sometimes intensify this longing. But fear not, for the world is filled with kindred spirits waiting to be discovered.

Overcoming loneliness on the road requires an open mind and a willingness to step outside of your comfort zone. The first step is to embrace the adventure and understand that making friends while traveling is not only possible but highly beneficial to your overall experience. By cultivating an outgoing and friendly attitude, you can attract like-minded travelers into your journey.

One effective way to meet fellow travelers is by staying in places that foster social interactions. Hostels, for example, are a haven for solo travelers where friendships are easily forged. Many hostels organize events, such as group hikes, pub crawls, or cooking classes, to encourage interaction among guests.

Attending these activities not only allows you to connect with others but also creates an opportunity to share your travel experiences and learn from theirs.

Engaging in activities and experiences that reflect your interests can also lead you to meet like-minded individuals. If you're a nature enthusiast, for instance, joining eco-tours, diving expeditions, or hiking groups will increase your chances of encountering fellow travelers with a shared passion for the great outdoors. This shared interest forms a strong foundation for friendship, making it easier to establish meaningful connections.

Furthermore, don't ignore the power of technology in overcoming loneliness while traveling. The rise of social media and travel-related platforms has made it easier than ever to connect with like-minded individuals. Numerous online communities cater specifically to solo female travelers, offering tips, advice, and even the opportunity to find travel companions. Platforms such as Travel Buddies and Girls LOVE Travel encourage solo travelers to connect and support each other, inspiring friendships that can transcend geographical boundaries.

While it's important to make efforts to meet fellow travelers, don't forget to trust your instincts and prioritize your safety. Always exercise caution and be selective about the people you interact with. Engage in conversations, observe body language, and never hesitate to distance yourself from any situation that feels uncomfortable or potentially unsafe.

By embracing the adventure, staying in social accommodation, participating in group activities, pursuing your interests, and utilizing online platforms, you can create meaningful connections that make your journey all the more enriching. Remember, travel is not just about the destinations; it's about the people you meet along the way. So, step out of your comfort zone, open your heart to new friendships, and let the magic of human connection unfold as you embark on your empowering solo adventures.

4.2 Cultural Immersion: Engaging with Local Communities and Building Bridges

Embarking on a solo journey can sometimes feel daunting, especially when visiting unfamiliar destinations. However, taking the time to engage with local communities allows us to break down barriers, embrace different cultures, and foster connections that can truly enrich our travel experiences.

Cultural immersion goes beyond merely observing and admiring different customs and traditions from a distance – it involves actively participating in local activities, meeting locals, and taking the time to understand their perspectives on life. This level of engagement can lead to a greater appreciation and understanding of the destination, ultimately leaving a lasting impact on both the traveler and the local community.

One way to engage with local communities is through volunteering. By dedicating our time and skills to meaningful projects, we not only make a positive contribution, but we also have the opportunity to interact with locals on a deeper level. Through shared experience and working towards a common goal, strong bonds can be formed that bridge the gap between traveler and local resident. Whether it's teaching English to local students, participating in conservation efforts, or lending a helping hand in community-driven initiatives, engaging in volunteer work allows us to see the world through the eyes of those who call it home.

Another avenue for cultural immersion is through homestays or staying with local families. This provides an intimate glimpse into the daily lives, traditions, and values of the local community. By sharing meals, stories, and experiences with our host families, we gain a genuine understanding of their way of life. This, in turn, helps break down any preconceived stereotypes or misconceptions we may have had and allows us to build bridges based on mutual respect and understanding.

Participating in local festivities and celebrations is also an excellent way to immerse ourselves in different cultures. Attending traditional festivals, religious ceremonies, or community gatherings provides a unique opportunity to witness age-old traditions firsthand. By embracing the local customs and joining in the festivities, we become active participants in the culture, forging connections and enhancing our travel experiences.

When engaging with local communities, it's crucial to approach interactions with an open mind and a willingness to learn. Respect for local customs and traditions should always guide our actions, as cultural sensitivity is key to building bridges and meaningful connections. By putting aside our own biases and preconceptions, we can create spaces for genuine exchanges that can enrich both our own lives and the lives of the locals we encounter.

By actively engaging with local communities, we can bridge gaps, break down stereotypes, and forge connections that enrich both our travel experiences and the lives of those we encounter. Whether through volunteering, homestays, or participation in local festivities, cultural immersion allows us to empower ourselves as solo female travelers, fostering a deeper understanding and appreciation of the world on our own terms.

4.3 Solo, Not Solitary: Finding Companionship in Solo Travel

Traveling solo does not mean being solitary. It is possible to find companionship and build relationships while embarking on solo adventures. These connections can come in various forms, from fellow travelers to locals who graciously offer their friendship. The key lies in the willingness to open oneself up to new experiences and embrace the unknown.

When traveling solo, it is natural to have moments of solitude. These moments allow for self-reflection and personal growth. However, breaking the boundaries of solitude and engaging with others can lead to incredible experiences and forge lifelong friendships. By seeking companionship, solo travelers can create bonds with like-minded individuals who share similar interests and passions.

One of the best ways to connect with others while traveling solo is through staying in hostels. Hostels provide a platform for meeting fellow travelers from all walks of life. Sharing dormitories, common spaces, and communal activities offer ample opportunities to strike up conversations and exchange travel stories. These interactions not only create connections but also provide valuable insights into different cultures and perspectives.

In addition to hostels, solo travelers can also find companionship through group activities and organized tours. These activities bring people together who have a shared interest in adventure, exploration, and cultural discovery. Whether it is hiking through breathtaking landscapes or joining a cooking class to learn the secrets of a local cuisine, these experiences foster a sense of camaraderie and create memories that last a lifetime.

It is essential to remember that connections made during solo travel can be fleeting, but they can still have a profound impact on one's journey. Sometimes, chance encounters or brief conversations can leave a lasting impression and remind us of the beauty and serendipity of travel. These connections can open doors to new destinations, insider tips, or even lifelong friendships that transcend borders and time zones.

While finding companionship in solo travel is undoubtedly enriching, it is crucial to prioritize personal safety at all times. It is essential to exercise caution, trust instincts, and be aware of potential risks when engaging with strangers. Women traveling solo should trust their intuition and opt for public spaces when meeting new acquaintances.

By embracing the chance to connect with fellow travelers and locals, solo travelers can enhance their experiences and create lasting relationships. Whether it is through interacting at hostels, participating in group activities, or being open to chance encounters, the connections formed during solo travel can empower and enrich the overall journey. Solo female travelers, armed with an adventurous spirit and an open mind, can find companionship in the most unexpected places and create experiences that shape their lives forever. So go forth, embrace the world, and create empowering adventures on your own terms.

Chapter 5: Mind, Body, and Soul: Nurturing Yourself During Solo Journeys

5.1 Self-Care on the Road: Prioritizing Your Physical and Mental Well-being

Traveling solo as a woman can be an incredibly empowering and transformative experience. It allows you to step outside of your comfort zone, explore new cultures, and gain a deeper understanding of yourself and the world around you. However, embarking on solo adventures also comes with its own set of challenges, one of which is the need to prioritize your physical and mental well-being. In this chapter, we will delve into the importance of self-care on the road and provide you with practical advice on how to nurture yourself during solo journeys.

As a solo female traveler, it is crucial to make your physical and mental health a top priority. While the excitement of exploring new destinations can be overwhelming, it is important to remember that taking care of yourself is fundamental to ensuring a positive and enjoyable experience. Neglecting your well-being can quickly lead to exhaustion, lowered immune function, and negatively impact your overall enjoyment of the journey.

Physical self-care involves paying attention to your body's needs and taking steps to maintain your physical health. Here are some tips to help you prioritize your physical well-being on the road:

- Prioritize sleep: Proper sleep is essential for maintaining energy levels and overall health. Make sure to establish a bedtime routine and create a comfortable sleep environment wherever you go. Invest in a travel pillow and earplugs, and consider packing an eye mask to ensure a restful sleep.

- Eat well: Exploring new cuisines is undoubtedly one of the highlights of travel. However, it is important to nourish your body with nutritious meals to maintain your energy levels. Keep yourself hydrated, pack healthy snacks, and try to incorporate fruits and vegetables into your diet.

- Stay active: Traveling can often disrupt your regular exercise routine. However, finding ways to stay active on the road is crucial for physical and mental well-being. Take advantage of the opportunity to explore your surroundings on foot, try local activities such as hiking or yoga, or simply find a gym or studio near your accommodation.

While physical self-care is essential, mental well-being is equally important. Here are some tips to help you prioritize your mental health during solo journeys:

- Practice mindfulness: Solo travel provides a unique opportunity for self-reflection and introspection. Take time each day to be present in the moment, meditate, or journal your thoughts and feelings. This will help you stay grounded and connected to yourself throughout your journey.

- Reach out to loved ones: Solo travel can sometimes feel lonely, but it doesn't have to be. Stay connected with your loved ones through regular phone calls, messages, or video chats. Sharing your experiences with those who care about you can provide support and a sense of belonging.

- Set boundaries: While it can be tempting to constantly seek new experiences, it is important to listen to your body and mind. Learn to recognize when you need downtime and set boundaries that allow you to prioritize your own needs. This may mean saying no to certain activities or carving out quiet moments for yourself.

By prioritizing both your physical and mental well-being, you will not only enhance your solo travel experience, but also empower yourself in the process. Self-care on the road is not just a luxury, but a necessity. Empower yourself with this guide and embrace solo female travel as an opportunity to grow, learn, and nurture all aspects of yourself.

By following the tips on physical self-care, such as prioritizing sleep, eating well, and staying active, you can ensure your body is in a good place during your journey. Additionally, practicing mindfulness, reaching out to loved ones, and setting boundaries will help you maintain your mental health on the road. By prioritizing self-care, you will have a more enjoyable and empowering solo travel experience.

5.2 Inner Reflection: Finding Peace and Balance in Solitude

In today's fast-paced, interconnected world, finding moments of peace and balance can be a challenge. We are constantly bombarded with information, distractions, and the expectations of others. In this chapter, we will explore the concept of inner reflection and the importance of finding peace and balance in solitude during solo journeys. As an avid traveler myself, I have experienced firsthand the transformative power of solitude and the deep insights it can bring.

Solitude is not to be mistaken for loneliness. It is a state of being alone, where one can delve into their innermost thoughts and emotions, free from external distractions. It is during these moments of solitude that we truly get to know ourselves and discover our inner strengths and weaknesses. Solo female travel provides the perfect opportunity to embrace solitude and experience the empowering effects it can have on our mental, emotional, and spiritual well-being.

When embarking on a solo journey, one of the first steps towards finding peace and balance in solitude is disconnecting from the outside world. In our everyday lives, we are constantly connected to technology and the demands of others. But when we detach ourselves from these distractions, we create space for inner reflection. By putting aside our devices and embracing the silence, we allow our minds to quiet down and our true selves to emerge.

During my own solo adventures, I have found that nature is the perfect setting for inner reflection. Surrounded by the beauty and tranquility of the natural world, I have been able to disconnect from the hustle and bustle of everyday life and truly connect with myself. Whether it's hiking through dense forests, sitting by a serene lake, or climbing a majestic mountain, nature provides a soothing backdrop that helps us find peace and balance within.

With solitude comes the opportunity to engage in self-care and nourish our minds, bodies, and souls. When we travel alone, we have the freedom to set our own schedule and focus on our personal well-being. It could be as simple as meditating in the morning, practicing yoga on a mountaintop, or journaling our thoughts and emotions at sunset. Engaging in these self-care practices not only rejuvenates us physically, but also allows us to gain clarity, release pent-up emotions, and find a deeper sense of peace within ourselves.

But inner reflection goes beyond self-care. It is a journey of self-discovery and self-acceptance. During moments of solitude, we have the opportunity to confront our fears, confront our flaws, and embrace our strengths. It is a time to process our emotions, reflect on past experiences, and gain insight into our true desires and passions. Through this introspection, we can create a stronger connection with ourselves and develop a greater understanding of who we are as individuals.

As we embark on solo journeys, it is important to embrace solitude and find peace and balance within ourselves. By disconnecting from the outside world, immersing ourselves in nature, engaging in self-care practices, and engaging in deep introspection, we open the doors to personal growth and empowerment. Solo female travel provides the ideal platform for us to explore our innermost thoughts and emotions, and to cultivate a newfound sense of peace, confidence, and self-awareness. So, fellow travelers, let us embark on our empowering adventures, armed with the knowledge that inner reflection is the key to finding peace and balance in solitude.

5.3 Mindful Travel: Connecting with Nature and Cultivating Mindfulness

This essay delves deep into the experiences of a solo female traveler, providing insight into the transformative power of immersing oneself in the natural world and harnessing the potential of mindfulness.

Mindful Travel: A Journey Within:

Traveling presents a unique opportunity to escape the daily hustle and bustle, offering a chance to reconnect with our inner selves. Mindful travel takes this idea a step further by encouraging travelers to engage deeply with nature and witness its wonders firsthand. With a keen focus on the present moment, solo female travelers can immerse themselves in the healing power of natural landscapes, fostering a profound connection with the environment and nurturing their mind, body, and soul.

Connecting with Nature: A Sensory Awakening:

The key to mindful travel lies in our ability to engage with nature through all of our senses. As a solo female traveler, I found myself drawn to remote places, where breathtaking sceneries awaited. The rhythmic crashing of waves against majestic cliffs, the gentle touch of a soft breeze on my skin, the vibrant colors of flowers swaying in the wind- these experiences left an indelible mark on my spirit. Engaging with nature stimulates our senses, allowing us to fully appreciate the awe-inspiring beauty of the world around us.

Cultivating Mindfulness: Finding Stillness in Motion:

As an advocate for solo female travel, I believe that mindfulness holds the key to unlocking our true potential. Mindfulness encourages us to fully engage with each moment, enabling us to let go of worries and anchor ourselves in the present. In the context of mindful travel, I found moments of stillness amidst motion. Whether hiking through vast mountains or meandering along serene lakes, the rhythmic motion of my body in congruence with the initial tranquility of nature allowed me to cultivate a sense of inner peace and mindfulness.

Nature's Wisdom: Lessons Learned along the Journey:

The natural world acts as a teacher and guide, imparting wisdom and life lessons to those who are receptive. When cultivating mindfulness during solo journeys, one begins to realize the interconnectedness of all living beings. Witnessing the harmony and resilience of nature instills in us a deep sense of respect and care for the environment. Moreover, these experiences teach us to appreciate the ephemeral nature of life itself, as seasons change and landscapes transform. Mindful travel empowers the solo female traveler to embody a mindset of stewardship, inspiring action to preserve and protect the places we cherish.

Mindful travel provides a transformative journey for the solo female traveler, offering an opportunity to connect deeply with nature while nurturing mindfulness. By opening ourselves up to the wonders of the natural world, we awaken our senses, find stillness amidst motion, and embrace the interconnectedness of all life. Through this chapter, we delve into the realms of the mind, body, and soul, empowering women to embark on adventurous solo journeys that lead to personal growth and empowerment.

Chapter 6: Cultural Sensitivity: Embracing Diversity and Respectful Travel

6.1 Cultural Etiquette: Navigating Different Social Norms with Grace

As a passionate traveler, I have embarked on numerous solo adventures, exploring the fascinating corners of our world. Along the way, I have been enriched by captivating cultures, diverse communities, and different social norms. 1: Cultural Etiquette. This chapter offers valuable insights on how to navigate unfamiliar social norms with grace, ensuring respectful travel experiences and empowering encounters abroad.

Understanding Cultural Etiquette:

When traveling solo, understanding and respecting the cultural norms of the destination you visit becomes a fundamental aspect of responsible travel. Cultural etiquette encompasses both verbal and non-verbal communication, dress codes, gestures, and other social conventions. Navigating these norms with grace is crucial for building positive relationships, avoiding misunderstandings, and embracing the true essence of a foreign culture.

Observation and Research:

One of the foremost strategies in navigating cultural etiquette is diligent observation and research before embarking on a journey. Learning about a destination's cultural norms, customs, traditions, and taboos in advance helps female travelers establish a foundation of understanding and fosters cross-cultural sensitivity. By studying guidebooks, exploring reliable travel resources, or engaging in conversations with locals, travelers can gain insights into the cultural intricacies unique to their destination.

Appropriate Dress Codes:

Dressing appropriately is an essential aspect of demonstrating cultural respect. Understanding the local dress codes and adhering to them shows consideration for local customs and religious sensitivities. Whether it involves covering shoulders, wearing headscarves, or avoiding revealing attire, respecting these cultural norms not only ensures smoother interactions but also promotes personal safety and helps establish a positive representation of solo female travelers.

Non-Verbal Communication:

Mastering non-verbal communication techniques helps one transcend language barriers and aids in fostering connections with the local community. Simple gestures such as a smile, nodding, or expressing gratitude in the local language can go a long way in establishing a rapport and displaying genuine respect. However, it is vital to recognize that non-verbal cues vary across cultures; what may be considered positive or polite in one culture might be perceived differently in another. Navigating this aspect necessitates humility, empathy, and adaptability to local customs and practices.

Local Greetings and Etiquette:

Cultural norms also encompass social greetings and etiquette protocols unique to each destination. Greeting locals in their native language not only demonstrates effort and appreciation but also portrays an understanding and respect for their cultural identity. Furthermore, being mindful of local customs such as removing shoes before entering someone's home or showing deference to elders showcases graciousness and appreciation for the local way of life.

Respecting Sacred Sites and Rituals:

When traveling to countries with historical or religious significance, respectful behavior at sacred sites and during religious rituals is imperative. It is vital to familiarize oneself with the practices and etiquette associated with these sites, paying attention to appropriate dress, photography restrictions, and maintaining a quiet and reverent demeanor. Displaying reverence for religious beliefs fosters harmony between travelers and the communities that invite them into their sacred spaces.

The exploration of different cultures and social norms is an enriching and rewarding experience. However, it is crucial for solo female travelers to approach these encounters with respect, cultural sensitivity, and an open mind. By observing and respecting local customs, dress codes, and etiquette, women can embark on remarkable adventures that empower not only themselves but also the communities they visit.

6.2 Challenging Stereotypes: Breaking Down Prejudices through Travel

By venturing out into the unknown, travel allows individuals to experience firsthand the beauty and complexity of different cultures. It shatters the stereotypes we may have built up through media portrayals or limited exposure, and instead presents us with a rich tapestry of diverse perspectives, traditions, and lifestyles. No longer confined to our comfort zones, we are forced to confront our own biases and assumptions, as we come face to face with the vibrant reality of the world.

Travel opens our eyes to the sheer variety of human experiences and challenges the notion of a "one-size-fits-all" approach to understanding cultures. Each journey offers a chance to meet people from all walks of life, individuals with unique stories to share and perspectives to contribute. Through meaningful interactions and conversations, we can break down stereotypes that restrict our ability to empathize and connect with others.

One of the most powerful ways travel breaks down stereotypes is by allowing us to acknowledge the inherent complexity and diversity within a culture. Too often, we fall into the trap of oversimplifying other societies, reducing them to a set of generalizations. But when we immerse ourselves in the everyday lives of locals, we discover that they too wrestle with similar challenges and triumphs, that their narratives are as varied as our own. The ability to see beyond the surface and acknowledge the diversity within a culture broadens our understanding and helps us realize that stereotypes are far from accurate representations.

Furthermore, by challenging stereotypes, travel provides an opportunity to dismantle prejudices that can perpetuate discrimination and inequality. When we witness firsthand the humanity behind those who have been unfairly stigmatized, the walls that separate us begin to crumble. We become acutely aware of the harm that stereotypes can cause and are compelled to confront our own biases. Through introspection and self-reflection, we can actively work towards breaking down these prejudices, both within ourselves and within society at large.

Travel also offers a platform for fostering mutual respect and celebrating diversity. By engaging with different cultures and embracing their traditions, we not only enrich our personal experiences but also contribute to a more inclusive and understanding world. As we learn and share our stories, we create a space that promotes dialogue, empathy, and acceptance. In breaking down stereotypes, we open up opportunities for collaboration, cultural exchange, and ultimately, a more harmonious global community.

By venturing out of our comfort zones and immersing ourselves in new experiences, we can confront our own biases, acknowledge the complexity of different societies, and actively work towards dismantling harmful stereotypes. Through these transformative journeys, we empower ourselves to become advocates for diversity and change, embracing the world on our own terms and forging connections that transcend borders and preconceptions.

6.3 Responsible Tourism: Supporting Local Communities and Preserving Culture

When it comes to supporting local communities, responsible tourism requires us to prioritize their needs and interests. One way to do this is by staying in locally-owned accommodations and eating at local restaurants instead of large international chains. By doing so, we contribute directly to the local economy, supporting local businesses and communities. This not only helps create employment opportunities for the locals, but it also ensures that tourism revenue is channeled back into the community rather than being siphoned off by global corporations.

Moreover, responsible tourism also means engaging with the locals in a meaningful way. This can be achieved by participating in community-led activities, such as workshops and homestays, where we have the opportunity to learn about their culture, traditions, and daily lives. By immersing ourselves in their world, we gain a deeper understanding of their challenges and aspirations. It is through these interactions that we can build genuine connections and foster mutual respect, breaking down cultural barriers and promoting understanding.

Preserving culture is another crucial aspect of responsible tourism. As travellers, we have a responsibility to appreciate and respect the cultural heritage of the places we visit. One way to do this is by adhering to local customs and traditions, such as dressing modestly in conservative areas or avoiding certain behaviors that may be considered disrespectful. By understanding and respecting cultural norms, we show our reverence for their way of life and help preserve their cultural identity.

Furthermore, responsible tourism also involves engaging in activities that safeguard the environment and promote sustainability. This can be achieved by participating in eco-friendly tours, supporting local conservation efforts, and minimizing our carbon footprint. By being mindful of our impact on the environment, we contribute to the preservation of natural resources, which are essential for the livelihoods of local communities.

As solo female travellers, it is essential to approach our adventures with understanding, empathy, and respect. By prioritizing local businesses, engaging with the locals, appreciating their customs, and protecting the environment, we not only empower ourselves but also contribute to the sustainable development and preservation of the places we visit. So let us embrace the diversity that the world has to offer and travel responsibly, making a positive difference along the way.

Chapter 7: Traveling on a Budget: Making Solo Adventures Affordable

7.1 Money-Saving Tips and Tricks: Budgeting and Cutting Costs

When it comes to traveling, budgeting is a crucial aspect that ensures your solo adventure remains affordable. Making smart financial decisions allows you to maximize the value of your trip and have more funds available for truly enriching experiences. In this chapter of the book "Solo Female Travel: Empowering Adventures for Women," we will delve into point 7. 1, which focuses on money-saving tips and tricks for budgeting and cutting costs. So, without further ado, let's dive into some expert advice on how to travel on a budget!.

First and foremost, planning your budget in advance is essential. Before embarking on your solo adventure, take the time to map out your estimated expenses. Consider factors such as transportation, accommodation, meals, activities, and incidentals. It's important to be realistic and factor in unforeseen costs that may arise during your journey. By having a well-thought-out budget, you'll be in control of your finances and less likely to overspend.

One effective method to cut costs while traveling is to opt for more affordable accommodation options. Traditional hotels can be quite expensive, especially if you're traveling for an extended period. Consider alternative options such as hostels, guesthouses, or even camping, depending on your comfort level. These alternatives can be significantly cheaper and provide unique opportunities to connect with fellow travelers.

Transportation is another area where you can save a substantial amount of money. While flights may often be necessary for long-distance travel, consider alternative modes of transportation for shorter journeys. Trains and buses are usually more budget-friendly options, especially if you book tickets well in advance. Additionally, exploring your destination on foot or renting a bicycle can save you money on transportation costs while allowing you to immerse yourself in the local culture.

When it comes to cutting costs on meals, one great tip is to embrace local flavors and eat at local eateries. Avoiding touristy restaurants can not only save you money but also provide a more authentic culinary experience. Street food is another excellent option as it tends to be delicious, affordable, and an integral part of the local culture. Proactively researching affordable dining options beforehand can help you find hidden gems that offer incredible value for money.

Activities and attractions are often a significant component of a traveler's budget. To make the most of your adventure while staying on a budget, prioritize free or low-cost activities. Many museums, galleries, and historical sites offer discounted or even free entry on specific days or certain times of the day. Taking advantage of such opportunities allows you to explore and discover without straining your budget.

To further control your expenses, consider the timing and duration of your trip. Traveling during off-peak seasons can result in significant cost savings. Flights and accommodation are often cheaper during these periods, and tourist attractions are less crowded. Additionally, longer trips tend to be more cost-effective, as transportation costs can be spread over a larger period. However, do keep in mind your personal preferences and limitations when deciding on the duration of your solo adventure.

While it's essential to stick to your budget, it's also crucial to leave room for flexibility. Sometimes unexpected opportunities or challenges may arise during your travels that require adjusting your expenses. By having a small buffer in your budget, you can adapt to these circumstances without feeling financially strapped.

By planning your budget in advance, exploring alternative accommodation and transportation options, embracing local cuisine, prioritizing free activities, and being mindful of timing and duration, you can achieve your travel goals while staying within your financial limits. Remember, empowering experiences shouldn't always come at a high price tag, and with smart financial decisions, you can embark on incredible solo journeys on your own terms.

7.2 Accommodation Hacks: Finding Affordable and Safe Places to Stay

When it comes to finding affordable accommodation, the first hack is to consider alternative options beyond the traditional hotel stay. Hostels are a popular choice among budget travelers, and many offer female-only dorms for added safety and comfort. Not only are hostels significantly cheaper than hotels, but they also provide a great opportunity to meet fellow travelers and build connections.

Another hack is to look for local guesthouses or homestays. These options often offer a more authentic and immersive experience, allowing you to truly immerse yourself in the local culture. Additionally, you can find private rooms in guesthouses at a fraction of the cost of a hotel room.

If you prefer more privacy, but still want to keep your expenses low, renting an apartment or a room through online platforms like Airbnb can be an excellent choice. Many hosts offer discounts for longer stays, and having access to a kitchen can further help you save money by preparing your own meals.

Safety, of course, is paramount for solo female travelers. To ensure your safety while finding affordable accommodation, it is crucial to do thorough research before making a reservation. Read online reviews from other solo female travelers or join online communities where you can ask for recommendations. By relying on the experiences of others, you can gain valuable insights into the safety and security of different accommodation options.

When booking a hostel, choose one that has a strong focus on security measures. Look for features like 24-hour reception, lockers for personal belongings, and CCTV cameras. If you opt for alternative accommodation options like guesthouses or homestays, make sure to verify the credibility of the hosts and read reviews from previous guests.

Additionally, it is important to consider the location of your accommodation. Choose a place that is centrally located, well-lit, and easily accessible. Being close to public transportation or popular tourist sites can also be an added advantage. Prioritizing these factors will not only help you save time, but it will also contribute to your overall safety.

Utilizing technology can also enhance your accommodation search. Numerous websites and apps provide real-time availability and competitive prices for various types of accommodation. By using these platforms, you can compare prices, read reviews, and even book last-minute deals that fit within your budget.

Lastly, flexibility is a key element when it comes to finding affordable and safe places to stay. Consider traveling during off-peak seasons or weekdays, as prices tend to be lower due to decreased demand. Keep an eye out for special promotions and discounts offered by accommodation providers. By staying open-minded and adaptable, you increase your chances of finding the best deals.

By considering alternative options like hostels, guesthouses, and rental apartments, you can save money while experiencing a more immersive travel experience. Prioritizing safety through thorough research, choosing secure establishments, and considering the location contributes to a worry-free stay. Utilizing technology and being flexible further enhance your chances of finding affordable options. Remember, with the right hacks and a little bit of planning, solo female travelers can conquer the world without compromising safety or breaking the bank.

7.3 Cheap Eats: Exploring Local Cuisine without Breaking the Bank

Everyone knows that one of the best parts of traveling is indulging in the local cuisine. The flavors, aromas, and textures of a destination's food can provide a memorable and authentic experience unlike any other. However, for solo female travelers on a budget, the desire to try new dishes often clashes with the worry of breaking the bank. Not to worry, though, because in this section, we will explore how to find cheap eats while still getting a taste of the local culture.

When it comes to hunting for inexpensive food options, a little research can go a long way. Before embarking on your solo adventure, take some time to familiarize yourself with the local cuisine by browsing travel blogs, food websites, and even social media platforms. These resources are a treasure trove of information on where to find affordable yet delicious meals that can help you experience a true culinary immersion.

Furthermore, make sure to consider the local street food scene. Often, the most affordable and authentic food experiences can be found at local street vendors or food markets. Not only are these options easy on the wallet, but they also provide an opportunity to interact with locals and gain insights into their daily lives and customs.

Speaking of locals, don't be afraid to ask for recommendations from the people you meet along your journey. Locals are usually the best source of information when it comes to finding hidden gems and budget-friendly eateries that may not be listed in guidebooks or online forums. Strike up conversations with locals, fellow travelers, or even your accommodation staff, and you're bound to stumble upon some culinary treasures that won't break the bank.

Another useful tip is to take advantage of the lunchtime menus offered by many restaurants. Oftentimes, restaurants will have special lunchtime deals or set menus that are significantly cheaper than their offerings during dinnertime. By opting for these lunchtime deals, you can still savor the local flavors without stretching your budget too thin.

Additionally, keep an eye out for local food festivals or events that might be happening during your visit. These occasions often showcase a wide variety of affordable street food and regional specialties, making them a perfect opportunity to sample the local cuisine in a lively and festive atmosphere.

Lastly, consider trying out local grocery stores or markets for budget-friendly dining options. Browse the aisles filled with local produce, pick up some fresh bread, cheese, and fruit, and voila – you have the ingredients for a delightful and cost-effective picnic. Not only does this allow you to save money, but it also gives you the freedom to create your own dining experience wherever you choose.

By conducting research, seeking out street vendors and local recommendations, taking advantage of lunchtime menus, attending food festivals, and exploring local grocery stores, you can immerse yourself in the flavors of a destination while staying within your budget. Remember, the joy of travel lies not only in the destinations we visit but also in the local experiences we embrace. So go forth, savor the local cuisine, and empower yourself through the richness and diversity of the world's food cultures.

Chapter 8: Navigating Challenges: Overcoming Obstacles on Solo Journeys

8.1 Dealing with Language Barriers: Strategies for Effective Communication

Travelling to different parts of the world can be incredibly exciting and eye-opening. It allows us to experience new cultures, meet new people, and gain a broader perspective of the world. However, one common challenge that many solo travelers face is the language barrier. Communication can become a significant obstacle when we don't speak the local language, but fear not! In this chapter, we will explore effective strategies for overcoming language barriers and ensuring effective communication during your solo journeys.

One of the first and most important strategies for dealing with language barriers is to prepare in advance. Before embarking on your trip, take some time to learn a few basic phrases in the local language. Knowing how to say hello, thank you, and ask for help can go a long way in breaking the ice and showing respect to the locals. Investing in a phrasebook or language learning app can be immensely helpful in this regard.

In addition to learning basic phrases, it's also essential to familiarize yourself with the cultural context of the country you'll be visiting. Understanding the customs and traditions of a particular culture can help bridge the gap between languages. For instance, in some cultures, it is customary to greet others with a kiss on the cheek, while in others, a simple handshake will suffice. Being aware of these cultural nuances can make your interactions smoother and more enjoyable.

Another effective strategy for dealing with language barriers is to use non-verbal communication. While words may fail us, gestures and body language can convey meaning universally. Learn gestures that are considered polite and respectful in the host country, such as bowing in Japan or placing your right hand over your heart in the Middle East. By incorporating non-verbal cues into your communication, you'll be able to convey your intentions and understand others better, even without a shared language.

In situations where verbal communication becomes challenging, utilizing visual aids can be incredibly helpful. For example, carrying a small notebook with pictures of common items and actions can serve as a useful tool for overcoming language barriers. You can point to the picture of a taxi or a restaurant and show it to a local if you need directions or recommendations. Additionally, technology can be a valuable ally in such situations. Translation apps, such as Google Translate, can help you bridge the language gap by translating words, phrases, or even conversations in real-time.

Furthermore, seeking the assistance of locals and fellow travelers can greatly enhance your communication experience. Locals are often more than willing to help you navigate through language barriers and make your trip more enjoyable. Engaging in conversations with locals not only opens doors for cultural exchange but also provides opportunities for language practice. Additionally, connecting with fellow solo travelers can lead to shared experiences, support, and potentially even language partnerships. Joining online travel communities or attending language exchange events can help you connect with like-minded individuals on your journey.

While language barriers can pose challenges, they can also result in unexpected adventures and delightful surprises. Embrace the opportunity to learn and grow through these experiences. Remember that effective communication is not limited to words alone but also encompasses non-verbal cues, visual aids, technology, and human connection. By employing these strategies and staying open-minded, you can turn language barriers into opportunities for personal growth and transformation on your solo journeys.

However, communication can sometimes be hindered by language barriers. By preparing in advance, learning basic phrases, understanding cultural context, using non-verbal communication, employing visual aids and technology, and seeking the assistance of locals and fellow travelers, we can effectively overcome these language barriers and ensure meaningful connections during our solo journeys. So pack your bags, embrace the unknown, and enrich your journey with the beauty of diverse languages and cultures. Happy travels!.

8.2 Transportation Dilemmas: Mastering Public Transportation and Getting Around

When embarking on a solo journey, one of the first challenges that arise is navigating public transportation systems. Each city has its own unique transportation network, and getting accustomed to these systems can be intimidating. Whether it's a complex subway system or an extensive bus network, the key to mastering public transportation lies in careful planning and research.

Researching the public transportation options available before arriving at your destination can save you a significant amount of time and stress. Online resources and travel forums provide valuable information on routes, schedules, and any important details you need to know about the local systems. Familiarize yourself with the names of key train or bus stops close to your accommodation or major landmarks that you wish to visit. This knowledge will enable you to plan your itinerary more efficiently and minimize the chances of getting lost or taking unnecessary detours.

Additionally, investing in a good quality map or utilizing navigation apps can be immensely helpful in mastering public transportation. Platforms like Google Maps or local transportation apps offer real-time directions, estimated travel times, and alternative routes in case of delays or closures. These tools provide an added layer of security and reassurance, enabling you to navigate unfamiliar cities with confidence.

While public transportation is undoubtedly a cost-effective and efficient way to explore a city, it is essential to prioritize personal safety. Solo female travelers might encounter unique challenges in this regard, but with the right precautions, it is entirely possible to travel safely and independently. It's important to avoid secluded or poorly lit areas, particularly late in the evening or at night. Trusting your instincts and being aware of your surroundings are fundamental aspects of personal safety. If you ever feel uncomfortable or unsure about a situation or a certain area, it is always best to seek assistance from a reliable source, such as the local police or a reputable transportation authority.

Another transportation dilemma faced by solo travelers is language barriers. Communicating with local taxi drivers or asking for directions can be tricky if you don't speak the native language. However, it's important not to let language barriers discourage you from exploring a city. In many tourist destinations, taxi drivers or transportation personnel interact with international travelers on a daily basis and are accustomed to overcoming language barriers. Politeness and patience can go a long way when trying to communicate, and learning a few basic phrases in the local language can make a significant difference.

When it comes to utilizing public transportation, it is essential to keep an eye on your belongings. Pickpocketing and theft are unfortunate realities that travelers need to be wary of, regardless of their destination. To mitigate these risks, ensure that your belongings are secure, and consider using bags with anti-theft features, such as concealed zippers or slash-proof material. Additionally, keep important documents and valuables in a separate, easily accessible pocket or bag, making it less likely for thieves to target them.

By researching public transportation options, utilizing navigation tools, prioritizing personal safety, and being mindful of language barriers and theft risks, solo travelers can master public transportation and effectively get around in any city. Empower yourself with this knowledge, and embrace the freedom and independence that comes with exploring the world on your own terms.

8.3 Solo Female Travel and Its Impact: Facing Societal Pressures and Stereotypes

Solo female travel has become increasingly popular in recent years, as more and more women are embracing the thrill and freedom of exploring the world on their own terms. However, this empowering trend is not without its challenges. In this chapter, we will delve into the societal pressures and stereotypes that solo female travelers face and explore how these obstacles can be overcome.

One of the most prevalent challenges for solo female travelers is the societal pressure to conform to traditional gender roles and expectations. Women are often expected to be more cautious, less adventurous, and more reliant on others for their safety and well-being. This stereotype often leads to a lack of support and understanding from family, friends, and even society at large. .

However, solo female travelers are breaking down these barriers by proving that they are just as capable and independent as their male counterparts. By embarking on solo journeys, women are challenging societal norms and expanding the boundaries of what is considered acceptable for women. They are showing that they can be strong, resourceful, and courageous, and that they have the right to explore the world and fulfill their own desires.

Another challenge that solo female travelers face is the perception that they are more vulnerable to danger and harassment. Sadly, this stereotype is often perpetuated by the media and reinforced by cautionary tales that are shared all too frequently. This fear is not unfounded, as women do face unique safety concerns when traveling alone. However, it is important to recognize that these risks exist for both men and women, and that with proper precautions and awareness, solo female travel can be just as safe as any other form of travel.

By highlighting the experiences of solo female travelers, this guide aims to dispel the notion that women are more vulnerable and to encourage women to embrace the potential risks and rewards of solo travel. Traveling alone allows women to gain a deeper understanding of themselves, to challenge their comfort zones, and to build resilience and self-confidence. It is through these experiences that they can truly empower themselves and defy societal expectations.

Another aspect of societal pressures that solo female travelers face is the pressure to conform to cultural norms and expectations when visiting foreign countries. Women often find themselves navigating unfamiliar customs, traditions, and dress codes, which can result in feelings of discomfort and insecurity. However, it is important to approach these cultural differences with an open mind and a willingness to learn and adapt. By respecting local customs and fostering a spirit of cultural exchange, solo female travelers can bridge cultural gaps and foster understanding and mutual respect.

By facing and overcoming these obstacles, women are challenging gender norms, promoting equality, and inspiring others to embrace their own adventures. Solo female travel is a powerful tool for personal growth and societal change, and it is our hope that this guide will provide the practical advice and encouragement that women need to embark on their own empowering adventures. So dust off your backpack, book that ticket, and get ready to explore the world on your own terms. The only limits are the ones you set for yourself.

Chapter 9: Embracing the Unknown: Embracing Solo Travel with Confidence

9.1 Stepping Outside Your Comfort Zone: Embracing Growth and Adventure

In the enchanting world of travel, where possibilities are endless and new horizons beckon, stepping outside your comfort zone is a transformative experience. It is an exhilarating endeavor that opens doors to personal growth, empowerment, and a deeper understanding of oneself. In this essay, we will explore the significance of embracing growth and adventure, focusing specifically on point 9.

1. The Essence of Stepping Outside Your Comfort Zone:

Ascending to new heights and venturing into the unknown require courage and a willingness to embrace discomfort. Stepping outside your comfort zone invokes a sense of liberation, as it shatters the boundaries that confine us. By relinquishing the familiarity of routine, one embraces the uncertainty and unpredictability that propel personal growth and adventure.

2. The Call of Adventure:

Adventure is an innate yearning that resides within every traveler's soul. The urge to explore uncharted territories, experience diverse cultures, and immerse oneself in the unfamiliar is a fundamental human desire. Stepping outside our comfort zones grants us the opportunity to heed this call, embark on thrilling escapades, and create lasting memories.

3. The Pathway to Self-Discovery:

When we venture beyond our comfort zones, we encounter challenges that test our resilience, adaptability, and problem-solving skills. This journey of self-discovery allows us to unearth aspects of ourselves that remained hidden in the confines of the familiar. It is through overcoming these challenges that we reveal our true potential and grow as individuals.

4. Building Confidence and Empowerment:

Solo travel, in particular, is a unique avenue for embracing the unknown and stepping outside our comfort zones. It requires self-reliance, independence, and open-mindedness, all of which contribute to building confidence and empowerment. Breaking free from the safety net of familiar companionship encourages personal growth, amplifying our abilities to confidently navigate the world on our own terms.

5. Embracing Cultural Immersion:

When we step outside our comfort zones, we expose ourselves to diverse cultures, traditions, and perspectives. Through immersion in unfamiliar environments, we gain a heightened appreciation for the richness and diversity of our world. This exposure fosters empathy, cultural understanding, and a broader worldview, leading to a more compassionate, inclusive, and enlightened global community.

6. Overcoming Fear and Embracing Resilience:

Fear often acts as a barrier to exploring uncharted territories and challenging our comfort zones. However, by actively choosing to face our fears head-on, we cultivate resilience and adaptability. Each conquered fear becomes a stepping stone to overcome additional obstacles, empowering us to push our limits, both in travel and in life.

Embracing growth and adventure by stepping outside our comfort zones is a transformative journey that invites personal growth, empowerment, and self-discovery. The book "Solo Female Travel: Empowering Adventures for Women" eloquently captures the essence of this chapter, encouraging women to embark on solo adventures, explore the world fearlessly, and create lasting memories. So, dear fellow traveler, let us answer the call of the unknown, open our hearts to growth, and dare to venture into unexplored territories.

9.2 Embracing the Solo Journey: Lessons Learned and Self-Discovery

Embarking on a solo journey can be a powerful and transformative experience for any traveler.

When setting off on a solo adventure, it is crucial to embrace the unknown with confidence. Stepping outside of one's comfort zone and venturing into uncharted territory can be both exhilarating and daunting. However, embracing this uncertainty is where the true magic begins. It is in those seemingly uncomfortable moments that we find ourselves pushed to learn and grow in ways we may have never thought possible.

As a solo traveler myself, I have had the privilege of experiencing these lessons firsthand. One of the most prominent lessons I have learned is the art of self-reliance. When traveling alone, you are solely responsible for your own well-being and decision-making. This level of independence can be empowering, as it forces you to trust your instincts and make choices that are in alignment with your desires and values.

Furthermore, embarking on a solo journey provides ample opportunities for introspection and self-discovery. Without the distractions of companionship, one can truly connect with their innermost self. It is during these moments of solitude that we can reflect on our lives, goals, and dreams, gaining a deeper understanding of who we are and what truly matters to us. Through self-reflection, we become more in tune with our passions and purpose, ultimately empowering us to live more authentically.

Another valuable lesson I have learned through solo travel is the importance of embracing vulnerability. Being alone in a foreign land can be both thrilling and terrifying. However, it is in these vulnerable moments that we open ourselves up to serendipitous encounters and connections. By letting go of our fears and inhibitions, we invite the possibility of new friendships, cultural experiences, and personal growth. Through vulnerability, we learn to embrace the unexpected and trust in the process of self-discovery.

In addition to personal growth, solo travel also provides an opportunity to challenge societal norms and stereotypes. As a female traveler, exploring the world on our own terms can be a powerful act of empowerment. Breaking the barriers of societal expectations and defying cultural norms allows us to redefine what it means to be a strong and independent woman. By fearlessly embracing the solo journey, we defy the notion that women need constant companionship for safety or fulfilment. We pave the way for future generations of female travelers, inspiring them to take charge of their own adventures.

Overall, the chapter on embracing the solo journey highlights the transformative power of stepping outside of our comfort zones. Through self-reliance, introspection, vulnerability, and challenging societal norms, we can embark on a journey of self-discovery and empowerment. The lessons learned on a solo adventure extend far beyond the external experiences – they penetrate into the very core of our being, shaping us into stronger, more resilient individuals.

So, for all the solo female travelers out there, I encourage you to embrace the unknown with confidence. Step into the world on your own terms, ready to learn, grow, and discover the magic that exists within you. The journey may be challenging at times, but the rewards of self-reliance, self-discovery, and empowerment are immeasurable. Let your solo adventure be the catalyst for transforming your life and paving the way for a future filled with empowerment and inspiration.

9.3 Empowering Yourself: Embracing the World on Your Own Terms

Traveling has always been an enthralling escape from the ordinary, allowing us to embrace the unknown and discover new horizons. Solo travel, in particular, holds immense potential for personal growth and empowerment. In this essay, we will explore this pivotal topic and uncover the transformative experiences that solo travel offers.

Embracing the World on Your Own Terms is all about shifting the power dynamics from societal conventions to personal choice. When one embarks on a solo travel adventure, it becomes a journey of self-discovery, enabling us to define our own path without external influences. Rather than conforming to societal expectations of what women should be or how they should travel, solo female travelers can create their own narrative, making it truly a journey on their terms.

Solo travel empowers women by providing an opportunity to step out of their comfort zones and confront their fears. By immersing ourselves in unfamiliar cultures, navigating foreign cities, and tackling unexpected challenges, we acquire a sense of self-reliance that transcends geographical boundaries. Embracing the unknown becomes a catalyst for personal growth, enabling us to tackle adversities with confidence and resilience both during our travels and in our day-to-day lives.

One of the most inspiring aspects of solo travel is the ability to forge meaningful connections with people from diverse backgrounds. By embracing the world on our own terms, we empower ourselves to engage with locals, fellow travelers, and global communities, contributing to a deeper understanding and appreciation of different cultures. These connections enable us to challenge stereotypes and break barriers, fostering empathy, compassion, and a broader perspective of the world.

A crucial aspect of embracing the world on our own terms is prioritizing personal safety. Solo female travelers must equip themselves with practical advice and strategies to navigate unfamiliar terrains confidently. In this guide, the book Solo Female Travel offers valuable insights and safety tips to empower women, ensuring their adventures are secure and fulfilling. By taking ownership of our safety, we enhance our self-confidence while embarking on solo journeys.

An empowered solo traveler is someone who accepts and celebrates their unique journey. As Marcel Proust once said, "The real voyage of discovery consists not in seeking new landscapes but in having new eyes. " By venturing into uncharted territories, we discover our own strengths and expand our horizons, enhancing our self-esteem and self-awareness. Embracing the world on our terms allows us to make an indelible impact, not only within ourselves but also in inspiring other women to explore and embrace their own solo adventures.

It gives us the freedom to define our own narratives, confront fears, connect with diverse cultures, prioritize safety, and ignite a sense of self-discovery. By taking the leap into the unknown, we transform not only as travelers but also as empowered individuals who can inspire others to embark on their own empowering journeys. Solo travel becomes a catalyst for personal growth, enabling us to explore the world on our terms and fulfill our innate desire for adventure, independence, and empowerment.

Printed in Great Britain
by Amazon